Charles Dickens'

OLIVER TWIST

a Full-Length Comedy Adaptation

Adapted by

Mickey Coburn

Copyright 1985, 2004 by Mickey Coburn Beaman

PUBLISHED by

HaveScripts

All rights reserved.
Oliver Twist, Copyright © 1985, 2004 Mickey Coburn

CAUTION: Professionals and amateurs are hereby warned that performance of <u>Oliver Twist</u> is subject to payment of a royalty unless written permission is given waiving such fee. The Play is fully protected under the copyright laws of the United States of America, and of all countries covered by the International Copyright Union (including the Dominion of Canada and the rest of the British Commonwealth), and of all countries covered by the Pan-American Copyright Convention, the Universal Copyright Convention, and the Berne Convention, and of all countries with which the United States has reciprocal copyright relations. All rights, including professional/amateur stage rights, motion picture, recitation, lecturing, public reading, radio broadcasting, television, video or sound recording, all other forms of mechanical or electronic reproduction, such as CD-ROM, CD-I, DVD, information storage and retrieval systems and photocopying, and the rights of translation into foreign languages, are strictly reserved. Particular emphasis is placed upon the matter of readings, permission for which must be secured from the Author in writing. Anyone receiving permission to produce the Play is required to give credit to the Author as sole and exclusive Author of the Play on the title page of all programs distributed in connection with performances of the Play and in all instances in which the title of the Play appears for purposes of advertising, publicizing or otherwise exploiting the Play and/or a production thereof.

Published by HaveScripts
An Imprint of Blue Moon Plays, LLC
1385 Fordham Road, Ste 105-279
Virginia Beach, VA 23464
ISBN: 978-1-943416-88-2

CHANGES TO SCRIPT

Copyright law prevents this script from being copied or altered in any way by any technical or digital means. There may be no changes made to the script including but not limited to casting or dialogue without permission of the publisher and/or playwright.

PERFORMANCE/READING OF SCRIPT

This script is licensed for production by blue moon plays. It may NOT be performed or read aloud in any way (with or without admission fees) in a classroom, around a table, in front of a non-paying audience without a performance fee, which varies.

For any performance, you must apply for and purchase performance rights: in class, in school, for educational purposes, for paying or nonpaying audiences of any size, as a concert reading or a staged reading.

Anyone receiving permission to produce the Play is required to give credit to the Author as sole and exclusive Author of the Play on the title page of all programs distributed in connection with performances of the Play and in all instances in which the title of the Play appears for purposes of advertising, publicizing or otherwise exploiting the Play and/or a production thereof. Author's name must be one-half the size of the title.

All performances and/or readings of this script, whether or not admission fees are required, must apply for and receive a Performance License. There is a flat 100 fee if you wish to live stream performance.

Special Considerations:

Small-group readings around a table or in the classroom:
- If you are planning to use this script FOR CLASSROOM USE, you must purchase scripts for the members of your class or group. These may be purchased as a downloadable PDF (class/group study pack) which may be printed for that class only.
- If you are a small group doing private play readings for YOUR OWN ENTERTAINMENT or for a SMALL SENIOR ACTIVITY GROUP, you must purchase the number or scripts required by the characters: these may be purchased as a multi-copy download which will give you a printable script that you may copy for that reading only.

Video Taping
One video tape may be made for archival purposes only.
Livestreaming
Livestreaming is permissible with an additional fee.
Digital versions cannot be added to a free or paid online library or website, in any format, with or without member access, without the publisher's permission.
TO PERFORM THIS PLAY

You must buy sufficient scripts for the cast + 3, apply for performance rights, pay the performance fee, and receive a performance license.

To purchase scripts:

- Purchase sufficient printed hard copies (one for each cast member, plus 3 for the crew) - an automatic 10 percent discount is applied to multiple printed hardcopies at the point of ordering.

  or

- Purchase a Multicopy PDF which allows you to print sufficient copies of this script (one for each cast member, plus 3 for the crew). Click Return to Merchant to download your printable PDF. A link to the download will also be emailed to you, along with a link to the application for performance license.

To apply for a Performance License, go to the Product Page of the play and fill out and submit the application form.

To pay the Performance Fee, simply pay the invoice you will be emailed when we receive your application for performance.

Your Performance License for your requested dates will be emailed to you. All scripts and licenses shall be obtained at Blue Moon Plays at www.havescripts.com

If you wish to make changes in the script of any kind, you must receive permission from the publisher or the playwright. Permission is usually granted readily when schools or theaters face casting problems and the changes do not affect the quality or intent of the original.

For information, visit www.havescripts.com;email info@bluemoonplays.com or call 757-816-1164

OLIVER TWIST

CHARACTERS

Oliver Twist: Young orphan 10 years old

Mr. Bumble: The Workhouse Beadle (Double as street person) Mrs. Bumble: His wife

Workhouse Boys: double as Fagin's boys

Mr. Sowerberry: The Undertaker/ Brownlow Charlotte:

Sowerberry's daughter/street person

Noah Claypole: Sowerberry's apprentice: Double as street person The Artful Dodger: About 13 years old

Charley Bates: Artful's sidekick Fagin: The entrepreneur scoundrel Fagin's boys

Nancy: About 16 years old

Bet: Nancy's friend, about 13 years old Bill Sikes: Villainous criminal Nancy's love

Mr. Brownlow: Elegant gentleman/Sowerberry

Mrs. Bedwin: Brownlow's housekeeper

Street people: One plus doubles Bow Street runners--Two

Old Sally Musician

SETTING

Victorian London—Street scene with inset of workhouse and two shops. Street can be played in front of curtain.

ACT I
Scene 1   London Street
Scene 2   Workhouse
Scene 3   London Street
Scene 4   Sowerberry's shop
Scene 5   Street scene
Scene 6   Fagin's den
Scene 7   Street scene

ACT II
Scene 1   Fagin's den
Scene 2   Street/Brownlow's parlour
Scene 3   London Street
Scene 4   Fagin's den
Scene 5   London Street
Scene 6   Street / London Bridge

ACT I Scene 1

(*MUSICIAN enters from house – accordion or concertina; In costume; strolls to stage; ascends. In front of act curtain. Spotlight on little boy, poorly dressed against the winter, holds a tin cup and sings a Christmas carol. Lights dim up as **Bumble** crosses with **Oliver** in tow*)

Oliver: Are we nearly there? **Bumble**: What's that? What's that? **Oliver**: Are we nearly there?
Bumble: (*stopping*) Sir – are we nearly there – Sir!
Oliver: Sir – are we….
Bumble: Hyumph! It is not fitting for a small boy to ask so many questions.
Oliver: But – I –
Bumble: (*swings his cane – **Oliver** ducks*) You must remember Oliver – that you are a pauper and an orphan –
Oliver: What's that, sir?
Bumble: What's what? What's what?
Oliver: What you said – an orphan – sir?
Bumble: (*swings his cane*) Don't you know anything? (*backing **Oliver** up intimidating*) You got no father or no mother – boy – and yer'll live at the workhouse with the other trash in yer similar condition – and be educated and taught a useful trade.
Oliver: But – sir –
Bumble: Not "But Sir" -- Thank you sir!!

Oliver: *(muttering)* Thank you, sir --
Bumble: *(jumping up and down angrily)* And do not speak again unless you are spoken to – *(dragging him along)* Come on now –

*(The **Caroler** comes up to **Bumble**, who threatens him with his cane and flings him out of the way.)*

Bumble: Hyumph!! Out a me way!!!

Act I Scene 2

(Music in. Curtain opens on the workhouse. There is a long table and bench, placed with wooden bowls. Also a soup table w/pot, etc. **Mr. Bumble** enters followed by **Mrs. Bumble**, the latter dragging **Oliver** behind her; she's followed by the workhouse boys who proceed to the table. **Bumble** takes up his station; **Mrs. B.** deposits **Oliver** next to **Bumble** and takes up her station at soup table)

Bumble: *(striking the floor with his mace)* Boys – This 'ere's Oliver Twist. Like the rest of you, he's come 'ere to be educated and taught a useful trade -- -- *(boys laugh sarcastically as **Bumble** strikes floor)* Enough! Or yer'll be whipped! Now – where's yer manners? Say – Good evening Oliver!!
Boys: Good evening, Oliver –
Bumble: That's better. There now – you've been made truly welcome –

*(He shoves **Oliver** toward the boys; **Oliver** takes an empty place at table; **Bumble** strikes floor; **Mrs. B.** removes her mop cap and puts on a chef's hat; **Boys** line up for food carrying their bowls. **Mrs. B.** Lifts large ladle – **Mr. B.** shakes his head and makes clucking sound. **Mrs. B.** picks up smaller ladle; **Mr. B.** – exasperated – strikes floor; makes roaring sound. **Mrs. B.** picks up tiny ladle. **Mr. B.** Nods approvingly.*

*The **Boys** are served and file back to table where the food is consumed instantly. **Mrs. B.** changes hats again and stands near **Mr. B.**)*

Boy 1: (*stage whisper*) We got to do something about this yer know –
Boy 2: This ain't enough to feed a flea –

(Boy 4 begins to eat his bowl)

Boy 3: Blimey! 'es eating his bowl. Someone's got to ask for more!
Boy 2: Let the new boy do it –
All: *(each in turn)* Ay! Ay! Ay! Ay!

*(They huddle around **Oliver** and whisper in his ear. **Oliver** takes his bowl and approaches the **Bumbles**; the whispers stop; the **Boys** hold their breath)*

Oliver: Please, Sir, I want some more.
Bumble: What?
Oliver: Please, Sir, I want some more ---
Bumble: More?
Mrs. Bumble: *(shrieks and begins to faint)* Moorrrreeee……*(She falls on **Bumble** who is trying to get to **Oliver** who begins to back away)*
Bumble: *(pushing Mrs. B. to her feet)* He asked for more!! *(He stalks **Oliver** who takes off over/under table, etc.)*
Bumble: Stop him!
Mrs. Bumble: Catch him!

(**Boys** *join the chase trying to grab* **Oliver**)

Bumble: Whip him!
Mrs. Bumble: Snatch him!
Bumble: (*screeching*) He asked for more……!
(*grabs* **Oliver**)
Gotcha!!
Mrs. Bumble: He's a bad lot! He's got to be gotten rid of immediately.
Bumble: We'll hang him!!

*(The **Boys** gasp)*

Mrs. Bumble: No, no Mr. Bumble – we'll sell him. Drag him off to the undertakers. He's been needing a boy -- *(to the **Boys**)* What are you gaping at? Out of here all of yer – go to bed –

(**Boys** *begin to run dodging* **Mrs. B.** *in attempts to exit while…*)

Bumble: (shrieking) He asked for more!!!

BLACKOUT

Act I Scene 3

(**Caroler** *at opposite side of stage;* **Bumble** *enters dragging* **Oliver** *behind him*)

Bumble: A trouble-maker – that's what you are. Never has a boy asked for more. (*stopping*) Fix your hat! Stand up straight – or he won't give me tuppence fer yer.

*(***Oliver** *begins to cry)*

Bumble: Well, of all the ungrateful and worst behaved boys I've ever seen *threatens with his cane)*
Oliver: No—no – Sir – I'll be good. I will, sir. It's just that I'm a very little boy and it's so – so
Bumble: So – what?
Oliver: So – lonely, sir – so very lonely. Everyone hates me. Please
– don't hit me again – sir.
Bumble: (*angered*) Hyumph!! Come along. The coffin maker's waiting. *(Drags* **Oliver** *off; the* **Caroler** *sees him coming and takes off)*

Act I Scene 4

(Curtain opens on undertakers shop. **Sowerberry** *is pacing;* **Bumble** *enters with* **Oliver**)

Sowerberry: Ah – here you are Bumble – and that's the boy.
Bumble: Liberal terms, Mr. Sowerberry – liberal terms. Five pounds even.
Sowerberry: What's his name?
Bumble: Oliver Twist.
Sowerberry: Twist, eh? Dear me – he's very small. *(pulls out a measuring tape and measures him)* 'Ardly five pounds worth.
Bumble: Why, he is rather small – but he'll grow, Mr. Sowerberry – he'll grow.
Sowerberry: I daresay he will grow – eating my food and drink.
Well, he'll have to do, I suppose. *(calling)* Charlotte, fetch this boy some of the cold bits that were saved for the dog. It hasn't been around since this morning so we might as well not waste them. *(to* **Bumble***)* Here's your five pounds, Mr. Bumble, and goodnight to yer.
Bumble: Goodnight, Mr. Sowerberry. *(to* **Oliver***)* You behave now Oliver – yer hear?

*(**Bumble** exits as **Charlotte** enters with plate of scraps which **Oliver** gobbles up while she looks on with curiosity;*

Sowerberry *chains door for the night)*

Charlotte: Are yer finished?
Oliver: Yes, m'am.
Charlotte: Yer bed's under the counter. You don't mind sleeping among coffins, I suppose? It don't matter whefer yer do or don't, there's no where else fer yer to sleep.
Sowerberry: (*exiting*) C'mon, Charlotte.

(They exit. Lights dim. **Oliver** *can be heard weeping softly under the counter. morning light washes in; a loud kicking is heard at the outside door.* **Oliver** *crawls out fromunder the counter and begins to unchain the door. A voice is heard.)*

Noah: Open the door, will yer?
Oliver: I will right away, sir. **Noah**: Yer the new boy, ain't yer? **Oliver**: Yes, sir.
Noah: How old are yer?
Oliver: Ten, sir.
Noah: Then I'll whop yer when I get in, you just see if I don't, workhouse brat. *(***Noah** *begins whistling;* **Oliver** *opens the door.* **Noah** *enters eating a large slice of bread and butter)*
Oliver: You knocked, sir?
Noah: (*eating*) I kicked.
Oliver: Did you want a coffin, sir?
Noah: You'll be wanting one pretty soon if you joke with yer boss that way. Yer don't know who I am, do yer, work'us?
Oliver: No, sir.

Noah: I'm Mister Noah Claypole and yer under me. Open the shutters yer lazy ruffian. *(he kicks Oliver)*
Charlotte: *(entering with a tray of food)* 'Morning, Noah. I saved a nice bit o f bacon fer yer from the Master's breakfast. Oliver, shut that door and take them bits and this 'ere tea and drinkit there. *(points to a corner)* An' 'urry up 'cuz yer gonna have ta mind the hop, yer hear?
Noah: D'ya hear? Work'us?
Charlotte: Lor Noah – why don't yer let the boy alone?
Noah: Let him alone? Why, everybody lets him alone. Both his father and his mother left him alone. I'm just givin' 'im a change, eh Charlotte – hee! Hee! Hee!

*(**Charlotte** laughs with him)*

Noah: *(with a wink at **Charlotte**)* Work'us!! How's yer mother? **Oliver**: Don't you say anything about my mother. She's dead. **Noah**: What did she die of, work'us?

Oliver: Don't say anything more about her – you'd better not!
Noah: Better not!! Well – better not! Yer mother was a nice 'un, she was – oh, lor! Yer know, work'us – it can't be helped now and of course yer couldn't help it then, and I'm very sorry fer it andpity yer very much. But yer must know, work'us, yer mother was a regular right-

down bad'un.
Oliver: What did you say?
Noah: A regular, right-down bad'un, work'us. It's a blessing she died when she did or she would have gone to prison or been hung – yes she would – (***Oliver*** *jumps up and throws* ***Noah*** *down; they fight)*
Noah: He'll murder me! Charlotte! Help – the new boy's a'murderin' of me! Help! Help! Oliver's gone mad – Charlotte!

*(**Charlotte** screams. **Sowerberry** enters; **Charlotte** grabs **Oliver** off of **Noah**; they battle. **Sowerberry** and **Charlotte** put **Oliver**, kicking, in a coffin; **Sowerberry** sits on it; **Noah** sputters and chokes)*

Sowerberry: Quick Charlotte – water for Noah -- (*She runs off;* ***Oliver*** *kicks inside the box;* ***Noah*** *groans; she runs in and pours the water on* ***Noah*** *who shrieks*) Yikes!! He wanted a drink – a drink!

*(**Noah** pulls himself together with nasty looks at **Charlotte**)*

Sowerberry: What are we gonna do, Charlotte, this Oliver's a dangerous character – he might murder us in our beds –

*(**Bumble** enters)*

Noah: The Beadle!
Charlotte: Mister Bumble….
 Sowerberry: Ahhh Mister Bumble…. **Noah**: Oliver's gone mad!
Bumble: Oliver?
Oliver: Let me out of here –
Bumble: I'll take care of this – Do you know this voice, Oliver?
Oliver: Yes.
Bumble: And aren't you afraid of it, Oliver?
Oliver: No!
Sowerberry: He's gone mad, Mr. Bumble
Bumble: It's not madness – it's meat! He's been overfed. That's what comes of being generous. The only thing to do is to starve him for a day or two until his wicked spirit calms down.

(*He opens the coffin and takes* **Oliver** *out*)

Bumble: Now, yer a nice fella, ain't yer…..
Oliver: He called my mother names.
Sowerberry: What if he did? No doubt she deserved what he said and worse –
Oliver: She didn't!
Charlotte: She did!
Oliver: You're lying you wicked girl! (***Charlotte*** *wails and cries; all surround her;* ***Oliver*** *escapes*)
Noah: Where is he?
Sowerberry: Who?
Noah: He's gone –
Bumble: Who's gone?

Charlotte: Oliver – he's run away –
Sowerberry: Five pounds worth run away? Five pounds of my money run away? After him *(Chaos as they clamber for the door)*

BLACKOUT

ACT I scene 5

(A week later; outside London. early morning; **Oliver** *enterstiredly; crouches on a rock or step & huddles against the cold.* **Dodger** *saunters in whistling; sees* **Oliver**. *He studies* **Oliver;** **Oliver** *looks up; returns the steady look)*

Dodger: *(crossing over)* Hullo my covey! What's the row?
Oliver: What? Oh – I'm very hungry and tired; I've been walking for seven days.
Dodger: Seven days? Oh, I see – escaping from the Beak.
Oliver: Beak? A bird's got a beak –
Dodger: My eyes – how green! A beak's a magistrate – the law – yer know. Ungry?
*(**Oliver** nods)* 'Ere –

(He unrolls a newspaper and gives **Oliver** *bread and cheese which* **Oliver** *eats)*

Where's yer mother?
Oliver: Dead.
Dodger: No father eifer? *(**Oliver** shakes his head)* Money?
Oliver: No.
Dodger: Got any lodgings?
Oliver: No. Do you live in London?
Dodger: Yes. Mos' a the time. I suppose you want some place to sleep in tonight, don't yer?
*(**Oliver** shakes his head still eating)*
Dodger: I know a 'spectable old genelman as

lives there wot'll give you lodgings for nofink and never ask for the change. That is – if any genelman he knows interduces yer. And don't he know me? Certainly do! Now – What's yer name?
Oliver: Oliver Twist.
Dodger: Twist? Twist, yer say? How'd ya come by that?
Oliver: No one knew my name at the workhouse and "T" was next in alphabet order. They made it up.
Dodger: A proper name it is, too. My name's Jack Dawkins. But me friends know me as the Artful Dodger. *(offers his hand)*
Oliver: Mr. Dodger.
Dodger: Mr. Twist . Come along now – as soon as its dark we're off to London –
Oliver: Are you sure the 'spectable genelman won't mnd?
Dodger: Fagin? Any friend o'mine is a friend o' 'is an' vicey versy – com'on then –

(Exit as CURTAIN OPENS)

ACT I scene 6

*(**Fagin**'s kitchen. A basement room, old & dirty; a table on which are a loaf of bread, bottle, several pewter pots, a candle in a bottle; and around which sit five boys the same age as **Dodger**, smoking clay pipes and drinking from tankards. A clothes line with numerous silk handkerchiefs; a hob fire with a frying pan in which sausages are cooking; several rough beds made of old sacks are huddled side-by-side on the floor; a bird in a standing cage. **Fagin**, with his back to the scene is turning the sausages with a toasting fork. We hear a whistle.)*

Boy 1: *(going to stairs and calling)* Now then –
Dodger: *(off)* Plummy and slam!
*(**Boy** 1 lets them in)*
Boy 1: There's two o' them –
Fagin: Who you got there, Dodger?
Dodger: Fagin, this 'eres my new friend – Oliver Twist.
Fagin: *(bowing)* I am very pleased to meet you, Oliver. It is an h'exceptional honor –

*(The boys circle around **Oliver** removing his cap, trying to pickpocket him, etc.)*

Fagin: *(sternly; bopping the boys with his toasting fork)* That's enough of that, gentlemen. We are very glad to see Oliver – very! Dodger, fetch a tub near the fire for Oliver. Charley –

take off the sausages – Eat up Oliver, eat up! *(As they all eat, seeing **Oliver** looking at the handkerchiefs)* I see you've noticed the pocket handkerchiefs. There's quite a lot of them, eh my dear! We've just put 'em up, waiting for the wash – the wash– eh, m'lads? That's all, Oliver.

*(**Boys** laugh. improvise jollity; MUSICIAN plays. **Oliver**'s head falls to his arms & he drops off. **Fagin** lifts him up & puts him on one of the sacks as the lights dim & the boys clear the table. Several boys lay down as well. **Dodger** & **Charley** exit. Lights change to early morning light. **Fagin** is stirring coffee in a saucepan, humming to himself; he pours a cup at the table; looks to see If **Oliver**'s asleep; checks the door; takes a small box from hiding place near the fireplace. He sits at table, takes out a gold watch from the box, and then another. **Oliver** lifts his head and watches.)*

Fagin; *(to bird)* Let folks call me a miser – It's all I have to live on in my old age. Is that a pretty thing, my dear? Is that – *(He sees **Oliver** sitting up; slams box closed; grabs the toasting fork from the table & darts toward **Oliver**)* Why are you watching me, boy – what have you see? Speak up boy – speak –
Oliver: I didn't mean to disturb you, sir. I couldn't sleep any longer, sir –
Fagin: Were you awake ten minutes ago?
Oliver: No sir –

Fagin: Five minutes ago? **Oliver**: Oh, no sir –
Fagin: Two minutes ago?
Oliver: Oh, no indeed, sir –
Fagin: Are you sure?
Oliver: Yes, indeed sir – I mean – no sir – I mean – no, I wasn't awake, sir.
Fagin: Good boy, Oliver. You're a good brave boy. I was only teasing you. *(picking up the box)* Did you see any of mypretty things, Oliver?
Oliver: Yes, sir –
Fagin: *(clutching box)* They're my pretty things, my dear. All I have to live on in my old age.
Oliver: Yes, sir. May I get up now, sir?
Fagin: Of course, my dear. There's a basin of water near the fire for you to wash in.

(**Oliver** *goes to the basin; as he washes his face* **Fagin** *stashes the box*)

Dodger: *(voice off)* Plummy and slam!! (**Fagin** lets him in. the other boys awaken & get up)
Dodger: *(entering)* Look what I found! (**Nancy** & **Bet** *enter along with* **Charley**)
Fagin: Nancy, my dear! And little Bet. Up – up – boys – Where's your manners – we have company!
Nancy: *(seeing **Oliver**)* Who's this tyke?
Fagin: Forgive my poor manners – ladies, this is our new and good friend, Oliver Twist. Oliver – Nancy and Bet.

(They curtsy.)

Oliver *bows; boys catcall and whistle)*
Nancy: Enough o' that. Look wha' I gotcha Fagin. Just sittin' by the road asking to be breakfast –

(She produces a sack of apples. Boys cheer. She & bet toss them to the boys who juggle, play catch, and eat them.)

Fagin: Good show, Nancy. Good girl, Bet. (to **Dodger** & **Charley**) I hope you've been at work this morning as well, my dears –
Dodger: 'Til we're ready to drop –

*(**Charley** pretends to collapse; **Dodger** catches him)*

Fagin: Up – up – Charley. What have you got?
Charley: *(producing several handkerchiefs)* Wipes!
Fagin: Very good ones, very good. And what have you gotDodger?
Dodger: Pocket books!! Two o' 'em! *(**Boys** cheer)*
Fagin: *(taking them)* Ahhh! *(looks inside)* Not as heavy as they might be – but a good start to the day. Good work, my dears. *(He hands them each a coin from one of the pocket books) (To **Oliver**)* Now wouldn't you like to be as

industrious as these fine gentlemen?

*(**Dodger** & **Charley** bow)*

Oliver: Oh, yes sir. ; But I don't know how to sew a pocketbook.

*(All laugh. **Charley** rolls on the floor with laughter)*

Bet: *(pulling **Charley** up to his feet)* Cut it out, **Charley**. 'E don't know about this monkey business if 'e ain't taught.
Dodger: Well, let's teach 'im.
*(**Boys** cheer)*

Fagin: All right, Oliver. School's in. Watch closely now.

*(**Fagin** puts snuff box in one pocket, wipe in another, wallet in another, spectacle case, stick pin; buttons coat around him; trots around the room like an elegant gentleman pretending to look into shop windows. boys take turns robbing him; when he feels the thief's hand he cries out. one of the others drags the thief off & fagin resumes trotting with great exaggeration while the next team tries. **Oliver** enjoys himself immensely – laughing, etc. all improvise cheers, boos, etc. **Dodger** & **Charley** swipe everything by bumping into Fagin. many apologies, etc. All cheer.)*

Nancy: Good show – Dodger – **Charley** –
Bet: Now it's Oliver's turn.

(All shout agreement, etc.)

Fagin: *(indicating **Dodger** & **Charley**)* These two are great men, Oliver – make 'em your models; follow their every move and you'll be a great man, too, one day. Now – *(puts handkerchief in pocket)* Is my handkerchief hanging out of my pocket, Oliver?
Oliver: Yes, sir.
Fagin: See if you can take it out without my feeling it as you saw the others do.

*(He waits. **Oliver** holds up bottom of pocket and pulls hanky out)*

Fagin: Is it gone?
Oliver: Here it is, sir.
Fagin: You're a clever boy, my dear. *(**All** cheer. **Dodger** tussles **Oliver**'s hair)*
Nancy: 'As Bill been around, Fagin? I ain't seen 'im fer days.
Fagin: Forgive me, my dear, but you're better off without. I've never understood what you see in Mr. Sikes.
Charley: It's love! *(faint)*
Nancy: Aw – cut it out, **Charley** – 'ow about a bit of a party before we go back to work?
Fagin: Get the jug, Dodger!

(Music in. They pass the jug & do a musical number. At end of song....)

Fagin: All play and no work makes Jack a poor boy!! Off with you, my dears, and don't come home empty handed.

(Boys put on scarves, etc. & begin to exit)

Nancy/Bet: Ta – everyone –

Fagin: Oliver – go along with Dodger. Do what ever he does and you'll make a fine beginning.
Dodger: 'E's a bit green, Fagin –
Fagin: That's why he's going with you, my dear. He has to start somewhere.

*(**Dodger** ties **Oliver**'s scarf around his neck; **Fagin** waves them off as the curtain closes. All cross in-one immediately. **Dodger** & **Charley** with **Oliver**)*

Dodger: Now, yer just stay close to us, Oliver, watch what we do.
Charley: After a few time, you'll get the 'ang of it.
Oliver: The hang of what?
Charley: D'yer think this is such a good idea, Dodger?
Dodger: Aw, 'e'll be all right, won't yer, Oliver? 'E can just watch today. C'mon now –
(They exit)

ACT I scene 7

(Curtain opens on street scene; three vendors – Bookseller, ribbon or lace merchant, chestnut man. **Nancy** *&* **Bet** *pretend to be buying.* **Two Shoppers** *stop at stalls. The four* **Boys** *sing the xmas carol holding hats out for coins. Two* **BOW STREET RUNNERS** *stroll the scene. An ambiance of xmas. An elderly gent,* **Mr. Brownlow***, stands looking at a book.* **Dodger***,* **Charley***,* **Oliver** *enter and meander about looking over the scene.* **Dodger** *sees* **Brownlow** *& stops his companions.)*

Dodger: There.
Oliver: What's the matter?
Dodger: That old cove at the book sellers?
Charley: He'll do.
Oliver: He'll do what?
Dodger: Stay back, Oliver.

(They slink to **Brownlow***, pick his pocket, & take off to above the vendors;* **Oliver** *gasps as* **Brownlow** *puts his hand in pocket noticing his handkerchief missing. He sees* **Oliver** *who backs away and runs)*

Brownlow: Stop!! Thief!!

(He runs after **Oliver***. All on stage begin to shout 'stop thief' including* **Dodger** *&* **Charley***.* **Oliver** *takes off into the audience with* **Brownlow** *chasing him,* **Bow St. Runners***,*

***Vendors, Shoppers**, **Dodger**, **Charley**;*
***Nancy** & **Bet** swipe things from unattended carts. **Dodger** steals purse from lady in audience. **Boys** return to stage. **Bow St. Runners** chase **Oliver** onto stage & catch him. **Mr.Brownlow** is there to shout)*

Brownlow: That's him! He's the thief!

CURTAIN ACT I

ACT II scene 1

*(**Fagin**'s den; **Fagin**, **Nancy**, **Bet** are playing cards & drinking from tankards. the 4 boys are asleep)*

Bet: But they're terribly long about it – somefin' mun' of 'appened.
Fagin: Cease your fretting, Bet, my dear. They can't have got into trouble. Dodger's in charge –
Nancy: The young 'uns awful green. There – I win again. Fill 'er up, Fagin.
Fagin: *(getting up & pouring from the pitcher)* You're wonderful lucky tonight, Nancy. *(hearing footsteps)* Why, how's this? Only two of 'em? Where's the third? They can't have got into trouble –

*(**Dodger** & **Charley** enter, pale & breathless)*

Where's Oliver?
Where's the boy?

*(They don't answer; **Fagin** grabs **Dodger** & shakes him)*

Fagin: Will you speak? What's become of Oliver?
Dodger: 'E got took away –
Fagin: Took where?
Dodger: The traps got 'im and this ole gent we robbed – 'e took 'im off to 'is 'ome.

Charley: It weren't are fault, Fagin –
Dodger: Come – le' go o'me, will yer?

*(**Bill Sikes** enters during scene; he stands ominously back, listening)*

Sikes: What are yer up to? Ill-treating' the boys – what's the game?
Fagin: Hush – hush – Mr. Sikes – don't speak so loud.
Sikes: Don't call me Mister – yer always after somethin' when you do – you know my name – out with it –
Fagin: Well, then – Bill Sikes – we had us a new boy caught on his first job today. I'm afraid he may say something to get us in trouble.
Sikes: Very likely! You're in for it, Fagin.
Fagin: I'm afraid – you see – that if the game was up with us – that it would come out rather worse for you than it would for me, my dear. *(A murmur from the group)*
Sikes: Somebody must find out what's 'appening and wot 'es said. If 'e hasn't blabbed yet, we gotta get 'im back. Who's gonner go fer 'im? *(They look around & stop at the girls)*
Fagin: The very thing – Bet will go, won't you, my dear?
Bet: Who? Me? No, I won't go.
Fagin: Nancy, my dear – what do you say?
Nancy: That it won't do so it's no use a tryin' it on, Fagin.
Sikes: What d'yer mean by that?
Nancy: I mean what I say, Bill.

Sikes: Yer the very person for it – nobody about 'ere knows anyfing of yer
Nancy: And I don't want 'em to neither. No, Bill –
Sikes: Are yer my girl or not Nancy –
Nancy: I'm yer girl all right, but I won't go, Bill
Sikes: She'll go, Fagin – **Nancy**: No she won't Fagin – **Sikes**: Yes, she will Fagin –

(He raises his hand to strike her; all gasp – he hits her)

Sikes: Yes, she will!

BLACKOUT

ACT II scene 2

IN-ONE
(*Mr. Brownlow enters; Mrs. Bedwin in shawl enters from other direction*)

Mrs. Bedwin: Oh, there you are, Mr. Brownlow. I was just coming to look for you. Oliver's feeling ever so much better. What a nice lad he is, Mr. Brownlow –
Brownlow: Ah, Mrs. Bedwin – here's the tonic from the chemist. *(gives her a parcel)* He's so pale and small. Did you notice Mrs. Bedwin, how much he looks like my daughter, Agnes?
Mrs. Bedwin: He does indeed, Mr. Brownlow. I like him very much.
Brownlow: I must confess I find myself strangely attached to the child. There's a chance, of course, that he's deceiving me. Perhaps he's a thief afterall.
Mrs. Bedwin: I can't believe that, sir –
Brownlow: We don't want to believe it, Mrs. Bedwin. But we'll see – we'll see. Well, we mustn't leave him alone so long –

*(They hurry off. Curtain opens on **Brownlow**'s parlour. A settee; small Christmas tree on a table; **Oliver** sits, all dressed up, looking out the window)*

Mrs. Bedwin: *(entering; carrying tea things)* Mr. Brownlow has returned from the chemist with the medicine the doctor prescribed. You

can have it with your tea so it won't taste bitter.
Oliver: Oh, thank you very much, Mrs. Bedwin. You've been so kind to me.
Mrs. Bedwin: Here now, drink your tea. I'll be back in a minute and we'll have a nice game of cribbage.

*(She exits as **Mr. Brownlow** enters)*

Brownlow: Well, you're looking ever so much better, Oliver.
Oliver: Thank you, sir.
Brownlow: Now, I think we should have a serious talk, my boy –
Oliver: Oh, please don't say you'll send me away sir – don't turnme outdoors to wander in the streets again –or be put in that awful workhouse again – please sir –
Brownlow: My dear child, I'll not desert you – unless you give me cause.
Oliver: I never, never will sir.
Brownlow: I hope you never will. Well, well –

*(**Mrs. Bedwin** enters with a parcel)*

Mrs. Bedwin: The bookseller's boy brought these by, sir.
Brownlow: Oh, is he gone? I wanted to give him some books to take back
Mrs. Bedwin: Send Oliver with them. The air would do himgood.
He'll deliver them safely.
Oliver: Yes, do let me take them for you, sir.

Brownlow: *(looking at **Mrs. Bedwin** & back to Oliver)* Yes – if you wish it, you shall. The books are on the little table near the door. You're to say that Mr. Brownlow sent them and that you've come to pay the four pounds ten I owe him. Here's a five pound note, and you'll bring me back ten shillings change. Can you remember all of that, Oliver?
Oliver: I won't be ten minutes, sir. *(he exits)*
Brownlow: *(taking out his pocket watch)* Now we shall see, Mrs.
Bedwin. Ten minutes; twenty at most.

(They sit on settee; lights dim. CURTAIN)

ACT II Scene 3
I
*(Oliver enters with parcel of books; **Two Passersby** cross; **Oliver** stops center to fix his scarf against the cold; **Nancy** enters & grabs him from behind)*

Oliver: Don't – let go of me!! Who is it? What do you want?
Nancy: Oh, thank goodness I've found him – Oliver – my dearlittle brother. You must come home directly – you cruel boy!
Oliver: Leggo of me – leggo –
Passerby: What the matter, ducks?
Nancy: Oh, ma'am – he ran away weeks ago and nearly broke his mother's heart –
Oliver: She's not my sister – Nancy – leggo me –
Nancy: Yer see – he knows me – oh, make 'im come home – there's good people –
Passerby: Why, the little scoundrel –
Sikes: (**Sikes** has been watching the scene; eating) What's goin' on 'ere? Young Oliver – come home wif yer sister –
Oliver: Help! Help! I don't belong to them – help me –
Sikes: I'll 'elp yer – what books are these? Stealing again are yer? *(**Sikes** gives the books to **Nancy**; picks **Oliver** up and carries him off)*
Sikes: Come on yer young rascal –

(All EXIT)

ACT II scene 4

*(Curtain opens on **Fagin**'s den; dimly lit. **Sikes**, **Nancy**, **Oliver** enter)*
Sikes: Anybody 'ere?
Dodger: Nah – we been gone fer 'ours –
Sikes: What are we 'iding in the dark fer?

*(**Dodger** brings up the gas lamp; lights dim up)*

Charley: Look – Oliver's back. Oh, look at his togs, Fagin – superfine cloth and the heavy swell cut – nofing but a genelman, Fagin –
Fagin: Delighted to see you looking so well, my dear. The Artful shall give you another suit lest you spoil that Sunday one. Why didn't you write, my dear and say you were coming? We'd have got something warm for supper.

*(**Charley** & **Boys** laugh; **Artful** has been going through **Oliver**'s pockets, pulls out the five pound note. **Fagin** takes it; **Sikes** snatches it back)*

Sikes: Hallo – what's that? That's mine, Fagin –
Fagin: No, no my dear. That's mine. You can have the books, Bill –
Sikes: If this ain't mine – and Nancy's that is – I'll take the boy back again...
Fagin: That's hardly fair, Bill –
Sikes: *(tucking the money away)* It's for our share of the trouble.

You may keep the books.
Oliver: They belong to Mr. Bownlow – he'll think I stole them.
Please send them back and the money –
Fagin: You're right, Oliver, he will think you stole them. He will! (*laughs*)

(**Oliver** *makes a run for the door, screaming for help;* **Dodger** *&* **Charley** *grab him.* **Sikes** *goes for him;* **Nancy** *pulls* **Sikes** *back*)

Sikes: Stand off from me or I'll split yer head against the wall – **Nancy**: The child shan't be harmed unless you kill me first – **Sikes**: Shan't be? (*He flings her across the room*)
Fagin: What's the matter here? **Sikes**: The girl's gone mad I think – **Fagin**: Keep quiet Nancy, will you – **Nancy**: No, I won't be quiet – **Fagin**: (*to* **Oliver**) So you wanted to get away my dear –
Sikes: Called for help – did you –

(**Sikes** *picks up his stick and starts toward* **Oliver**. **Nancy** *jumps in front of* **Sikes**, *grabs the stick & tosses it away*)

Nancy: I won't stand by and see it done – you've got the boy now – let him be. Let him be or I'll put my mark on some of you –
Fagin: Why, Nancy – (*laughs*) You're acting beautifully tonight.
What an actress –

Nancy: Take care I don't overdo it. You'll be the worse for it, Fagin— if I 'ave to go to prison with yer.
Sikes: You're a nice one – so gen-teel of a sudden – to be a "friend" to the "child."
Nancy: God help me I am. It's bad enough he'll be a thief and all
that's bad from this night on. He don't 'ave to be whipped, too –

*(She goes to **Bet** crying)*

(to **Fagin**) I've thieved fer yer 12 years – since I was a child younger than him. You got him now – isn't that enough fer yer?
Sikes: I'll tell yer wot – Fagin – I'll take the boy wif me. Yer got Dodger and Charley and these offers. I need 'un this size fer a job I got to do. Dodger – get 'im out 'o them togs – I'll be back fer him tomorrow. All right – Fagin?
Fagin: Always the way – the man against the child for a bag ofgold!
Sikes: Comin' Nancy? *(she doesn't answer)* Agggghhhhh

(he exits)

Fagin: (to **Oliver**) It's all right, my dear. Get some sleep. It'll be better in the morning.

*(**Oliver** turns to **Nancy** for help.)*

BLACKOUT

ACT II Scene 5

(**Mr. Brownlow** enters; **Mrs. Bedwin** enters, running behind him)

Mrs. Bedwin: But it's so awfully late, sir – and such a cold night.
Brownlow: I must find Oliver, Mrs. Bedwin. Something terrible has happened to him – I know it.
Mrs. Bedwin: But ;Mr. Brownlow, it's still possible he was deceiving us –
Brownlow: It's possible. But somehow I cannot believe it. Go back into the house, Mrs. Bedwin, lest he comes home and no one is there –
Mrs. Bedwin: Yes, sir. Take care, sir.

(Exit in opposite directions. CURTAIN OPENS on the street; **Brownlow** *enters; two or three PEOPLE hurry by carryingXmas packages)*

Brownlow: *(stopping a passerby)* Beg pardon, sir, I'm looking for a young boy –

*(***Bumble*** enters in nightshirt, night cap with hat & coat over; dragging* **Old Sally** *with him)*

Sally: I can't go no farther, Mr. Bumble –
Bumble: It's not much farther, old girl – we've tracked this Oliver Twist to the home of one Mr. Brownlow – you must tell him the story you told

me tonight. There'll be a reward in it – I'm sure –

***(Brownlow** overhears & approaches **Bumble**)*
Brownlow: I couldn't help overhearing. I'm Mr. Brownlow. You have information regarding Oliver Twist?
Bumble: Bumble is my name sir. Beadle of the workhouse where Oliver Twist was well cared for –
Brownlow: Do you know where the boy is now?
Bumble: No, sir. But this old woman – Old Sally she's called – she come to me tonight with important information – go on – tell the gent what you tole me –
Brownlow: Please Sally – what do you know?
Sally: I'm a dying woman, sir. An' I can't die a'peace without the truth be know –
Brownlow: Go on – what is the truth?
Sally: Once I nursed a pretty young girl – she was sick 'an 'erfeet was cut from walking. She gave birth to a baby boy and she died.
Brownlow: What about her?
Sally: I robbed her – I stole this locket from around her neck –'ere it is –
Brownlow: *(takes it)* Agnes – it belonged to my daughter, Agnes--- The boy's name –
Sally: They called 'im –
Brownlow: Yes?
Sally: Oliver --- *(she dies)*
Bumble: I thought you'd want to know this, sir, if there's a reward—

Brownlow: A reward, Bumble? Take this poor unfortunate woman to the undertakers – the same undertaker to whom you sold Oliver Twist. Sold! Indeed! You will see that she has a proper burial – and I will see that you are removed from the workhouse and the children there given proper care ---
Bumble: But – but – but –
Brownlow: Go at once! Before I call for the police –

*(**Bumble** picks up **SAllY** & exits as **Mrs. Bedwin** enters)*

Mrs. Bedwin: Mr. Brownlow – a young woman came to the door – she said she had come about Oliver. She said you should meet her at London Bridge at midnight.
Brownlow: It's almost that now. I must hurry –
Mrs. Bedwin: Do you think it's safe sir? She was hardly a proper girl –
Brownlow: Mrs. Bedwin Look at this locket – you see who it is?
Mrs. Bedwin: Why sir, it's Miss Agnes.
Brownlow: Yes, my daughter Agnes. And I have every reason to believe Oliver is her child.
Mrs. Bedwin: Oh, sir –
Brownlow: I must go and fetch my grandson safely home.

(Exit as CURTAIN CLOSES)

ACT II scene 6

(*A clock strikes to 12 during the following:* **Nancy** *crosses with* **Oliver**; *looks over her shoulder, hurries along;* **Sikes** *crosses after her, carrying his stick & looking fierce;* **Dodger** & **Charley**, **Bet** & **Boys** *cross trying not to be seen;* **Fagin** *crosses with his little box, slinking.* CURTAIN OPENS. *London Bridge. It's snowing.* **Nancy** & **Oliver** *enter;* **Sikes** *enters from the other side.*)

Nancy: Bill – (*pushes* **Oliver** *behind her*) Let him go, Bill. 'Es done no 'arm –
Sikes: What 'ave you done now, Nancy?
Nancy: I 'aven't done no 'arm Bill – I wouldn't say nothing to 'urtyer
– I only meant to save one boy –
Sikes: I do what I 'ave to do –
Nancy: Bill – why do you look like that at me?

(**Brownlow** *enters below the bridge*)

Brownlow: Oliver!!

(**Nancy** *pushes* **Oliver** *away & he runs to* **Brownlow**; **Sikes** *lifts his club striking* **Nancy**; *she falls to the floor of the bridge*)

Brownlow: Help!! Help!! Murder!! Help!!
(**Dodger**, **Charley**, **Bet**, **Boys** *enter; see* **Nancy**) **Dodger**: He's killed Nancy –

(Bet goes to her crying)

Charley: There he is –
Boys: Get him!! Stop him!! (etc.)

*(They storm **Sikes**; a whistle is heard; POLICE arrive; the youngsters back **Sikes** off the bridge; he screams; falls)*

Officer 1: All right now – we'll take it from 'ere—
Officer 2: We've been looking for you boys – where's this Fagin you work fer?
Dodger: We don't know no Fagin – do we boys?
Boys: Nah – Fagin? Never 'eard 'o him. What 'e talkin' about? (etc.)

*(**Mrs. Bedwin** enters; **Oliver** runs to her)*

Mrs. Bedwin: My dear boy –
Brownlow: It's all right now, Oliver. Everything is going to be just fine from now on.

*(POLICE approach **Brownlow**)*

Officer 2: Can you give us a statement sir? You saw the 'ole incident.

*(Crowd around **Nancy**; **Officer** talking with **Brownlow** & **Bedwin**; **Dodger** & **Boys** carry **Nancy** off; **Fagin** steals out of the shadows; looks at **Oliver**)*

Oliver: Mr. Fagin –
Fagin: Shhhhh ---
Oliver: Goodbye Mr. Fagin. I have chance to start over. I hope you will, too.
Fagin: Goodbye, Oliver Twist. I've learned a hard lesson – good-luck to us both. *(he sneaks off)*
Brownlow: Who was that, Oliver? What did he want?
Oliver: A poor and lonely man, sir. He was lost and I gavehim directions. Can we go home now, Sir?
Brownlow: Yes, Oliver, home –

(Music. **Carolers** *enter; all sing; curtain calls)*

CURTAIN

www.ingramcontent.com/pod-product-compliance
Lightning Source LLC
Chambersburg PA
CBHW071801040426
42446CB00012B/2665